# The Simple Living Series
## Practical Money Saving Tips
## By Marlene Stevens

ISBN 9781520879840

For John and Jack,
the most important people in my life.

# Preface

I am a wife and a mother who loves a bargain and is always out to seek a good deal. I love gardening, baking & cooking, nature/wildlife, photography, car boot sales, and charity shops. As a family, we love living the thrifty/frugal lifestyle which means we can afford a nice day out or a holiday, which is very important to us.

I'm writing this book because I want to share my money saving tips with you, hoping that it will help you save those pennies to help you reach your financial goals.

To do this, I have listed over 300 helpful and easy money saving tips for you to follow.

# Contents

# Introduction

With the high cost of living many of us are left struggling to make ends meet. Others may be trying to pay off debts, whilst some are trying to save for a major purchase like a deposit for a house, a wedding or maybe a new car or holiday. In order to save or live frugally you will need to get by as cheaply as you can and cut back on all luxuries. Saving money will require you to make sacrifices. You will need to understand the difference between essential and non-essential spending.

Start off gradually by cutting back in certain areas, keep looking for ways to cut costs and also look for ways to bring more money into the home. By cutting costs and saving money you will be able to get out of debt sooner than expected or will reach your savings goal quicker, or just be able to make everyday living a little easier. Stop spending and start saving and your goal will soon be in sight.

This book is full of practical tips to help you reduce your everyday living costs.

The first tip for you is to stay positive and keep focused.

# Water

A shower uses a lot less water than a bath.

If you do have a bath, save the water for flushing the toilet.

Use a shower timer.

Or have a "Navy Shower"
- Turn the shower on, get wet.
- Turn the shower off.
- Wash your hair and body.
- Turn the shower on to rinse quickly.
- Job done.

Take a look at your shower head... "Power Showers" can easily use more water than a bath.
- Aerated shower heads reduce the amount of water in the flow but maintain the pressure and just produce a steady and even spray.
- Low flow shower heads will reduce the amount of water that is used and still give you the full feel of a normal shower.

So just by changing the shower head you can save money and can still have a nice shower.

Most Water Companies give away free water saving devices, so this is certainly worth looking into.

Whilst the water is getting hot, don't just let it run down the drain, use a bucket or jug and save it.

Don't leave the tap running whilst cleaning your teeth.

Most flushes now have a dual flush option, so you can choose a shorter flush.

You know the saying – if it's brown flush it down, if it's yellow let it mellow. You can have a few number ones before flushing.

Put tissues in the rubbish bin instead of flushing them.

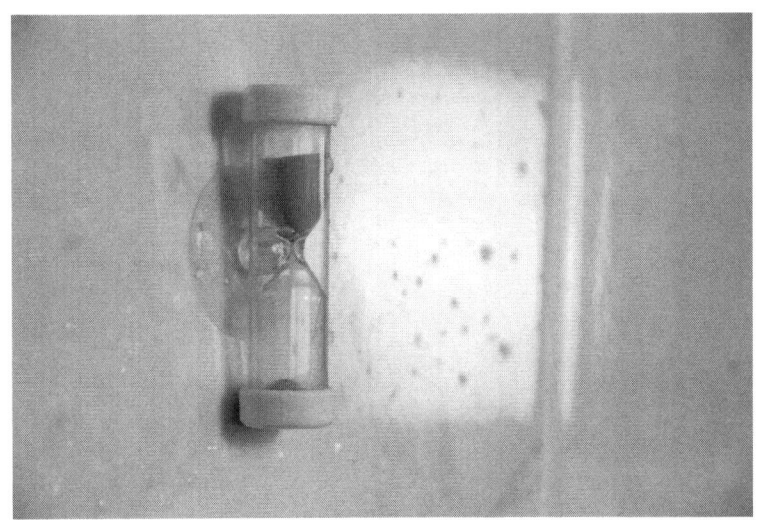

A four-minute shower timer.

Saving perfectly good water to flush the toilet with.

When you do need to use the flush, use the shorter flush option.

If you have a dishwasher use it, a common misconception is that dishwashers use more water, in fact these machines can be good water savers. Modern models use very little water, even less than washing by hand.

Avoid pre-rinsing dishes, just scrape them well.

Use the eco cycle on the dishwasher.

If you have a drink, don't just put the cup in the dishwasher, it can be used several times throughout the day, saving on the washing up.

Leave any dirty pots and pans soaking in a little soapy water, rather than having the tap running while you scrape them clean.

Use a shorter cycle on the washing machine.

If any of your clothes are really stained or dirty, leave soaking overnight, then you can still use a shorter wash, rather than using a pre-wash and/or a longer wash. (Don't forget to save the water you used for soaking the clothing for flushing the toilet.)

If you don't have much washing, do a hand wash, you will only need to spin it in the machine.

Reuse your towels, wash after several uses.

Only use the dishwasher and washing machine when full.

Only fill the kettle with the amount of water required.

The water from steaming or boiling vegetables can be used to make stock or gravy.

The water from boiled eggs when cooled can be used for watering the houseplants.

Wash your fruit and veg in a little water in a bowl, instead of washing under a running tap.

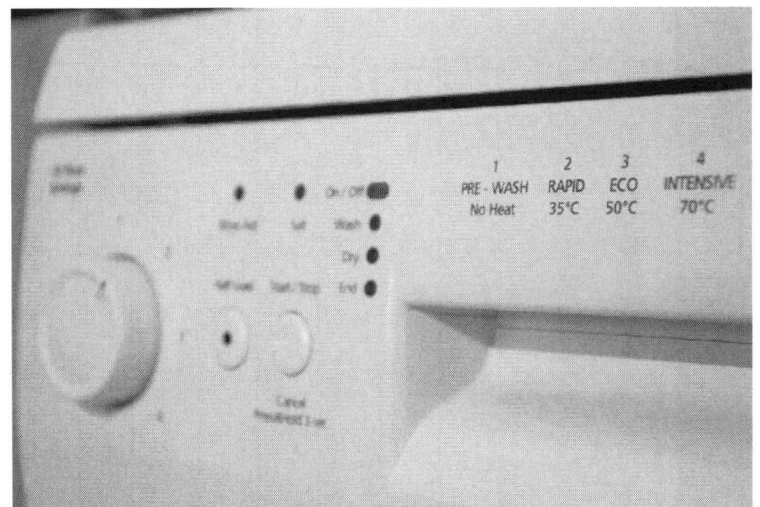

Use a short, cool cycle on the dishwasher.

Soaking any soiled garments means you can use a shorter wash cycle.

Using the lids on saucepans reduces the amount of water lost, so therefore you won't have to put so much in. It also helps your food cook quicker.

Select the correct pan size for steaming or boiling, larger pans will use more water than necessary.

If you are out and about even if you are just popping to the supermarket, use the toilets, saving you on water, toilet roll and hand soap.

If you use a hose nozzle for washing the car, turn off the water while you are shampooing your car, this can save you up to 100 gallons a time.

Use free water - water from the water butt in the garden can be used to wash the car.

Fix all dripping taps right away. One drip every second could add up to five gallons a day.

Make sure you know where your master shut off valve is located, if a pipe were to burst this could save gallons of water as well as preventing any damage.

This pan is too big!

Just right.

Putting a lid on helps reduce cooking time.

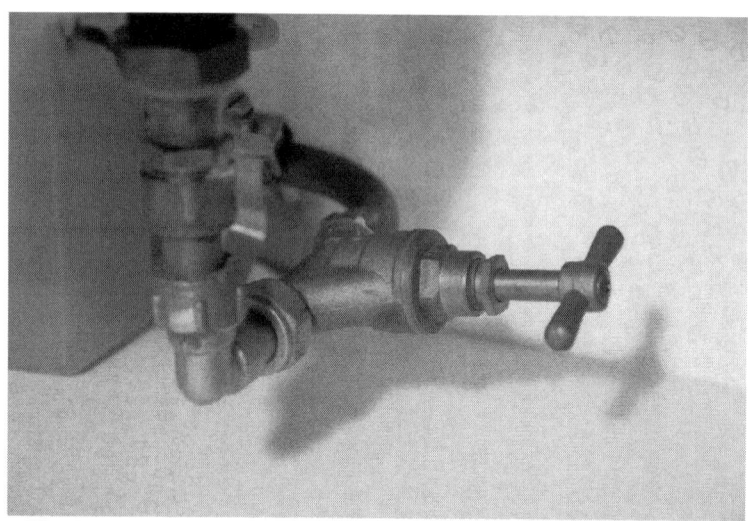
Find your shut-off valve so you can turn the water
off if there is a leak/emergency.

# Energy

Use low-energy light bulbs.

If you are sat watching the television, switch the lights off.

Pull the curtains as soon as it gets dark to keep the heat in.

Keep any draughts out by using thicker curtains in Winter, and if there is a draught coming from under the door, use a draught excluder.

Cut down on hoovering.

Use insulation sheets behind radiators.

Insulate the loft.

Insulate the water tank.

Switch those lights off and open the curtains as soon as it gets light.

Go to bed earlier, saving on lights, heating, TV, computer, drinks etc.

Do less ironing.

When buying a new appliance, check the energy rating – ratings A to C are the most efficient.

Turn down the thermostat by a degree or two – you won't even notice.

Switch off appliances when not in use.

If you are feeling cold, don't just flick the switch, wrap up warmer.

Switch off those lights when you're not in the room.

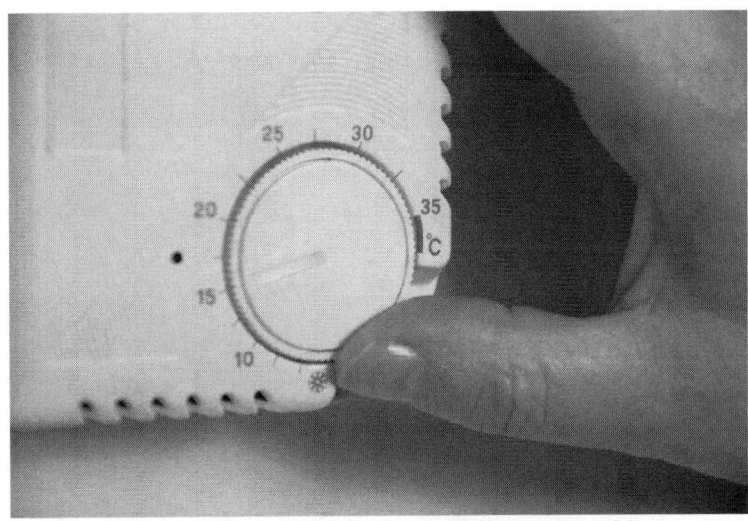

Turn down the heating by a degree-or-two. You
won't even notice the difference!

In the winter watch more TV in bed, snuggling up will keep you warmer, therefore you won't have to use so much heat.

If you have cheap overnight electric, take advantage of it – put the washing machine on etc. You don't have to stay up all night, use a timer.

No need for electric blankets, just use a good old fashioned hot water bottle.

Stop using the tumble dryer – use a clothes airer and dry around the heater or fire in the colder months. Check the weather and plan your washing around good days. Fresh air is free.

If you insist on using your tumble dryer, buy some tumble drying balls – these lift and separate the washing and allow air to flow more efficiently, therefore saving drying time.

Popping a dry towel in the tumble dryer will decrease drying time.

When the oven is already on, fill up any empty shelves by doing some baking or make some extra meals.

Leave the oven door open after cooking, allowing the warm air to circulate and help warm the kitchen a little.

Switch off the oven for the last ten minutes of cooking time.

Clean the coils at the back of the fridge/freezer every now and then to improve efficiency.

Put a metal skewer through the meat when roasting, it will cook the meat much faster if the heat can transfer to the middle.

Use a slow cooker.

If you have a fire or woodburner as your source of heat, look out for free firewood.

If you have a microwave, use it more often – they use a lot less energy than a cooker.

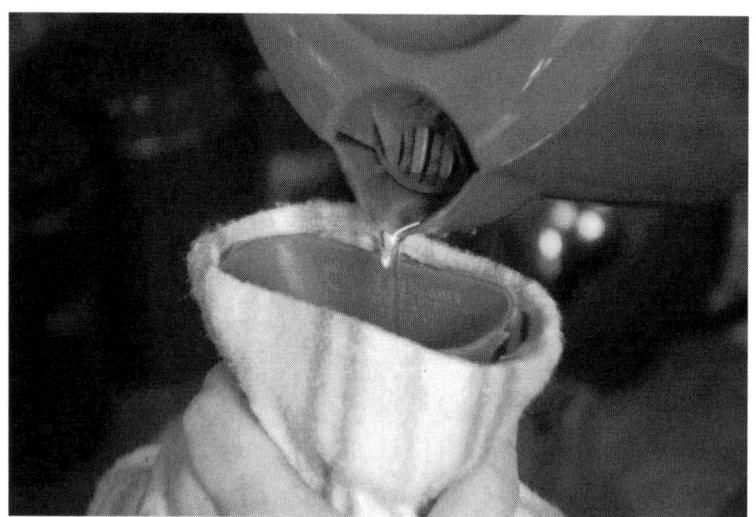

No need for an electric blanket – just use a good old fashioned hot water bottle!

Hang those clothes out to dry – stop using the tumble dryer, fresh air is free!

Keep the freezer full – it's cheaper to run a full freezer than an empty one.

Spend a day batch cooking for the freezer.

Instead of using multiple saucepans, use a steamer.

Charge your mobile phone in the USB point whilst using your computer.

OR

Charge your mobile phone in the car.

Combining your phone, TV and internet services could mean you end up paying a lot less.

Check energy tariffs – you could be paying more than you need to. It's really not that difficult!

Don't just cook one meal at a time – cook extra for the freezer, saving time and money.

Use a steamer instead of multiple pans.

# Food and Shopping

Go yellow sticker shopping – get to know when your supermarket reduces to clear, this can save you a huge amount of money.

Buying sachets of creamed coconut and watering down as instructed can work out cheaper than a can of coconut milk.

Know what is in your cupboards.

Grate cheese, it goes a lot further, you don't need a great big wedge in a sandwich.

Try making yogurt, it is very easy.

Use one tea bag for two cups.

Use frozen veg, it is better value for money and they are full of nutrients. Fresh vegetables lose nutrients after harvesting.

Try frozen berries.

Check out the Asian supermarkets, spices for example can be bought in bigger and better value packs.

Stop buying jars and packets of baby food – make your own.

Instead of buying pre-sliced meats, cook your own, you will get so much more for your money.

Use those leftovers, don't waste a single thing.

Save the olive oil from jars of antipasto.

If you use lots of potatoes, it is cheaper to buy a big sack.

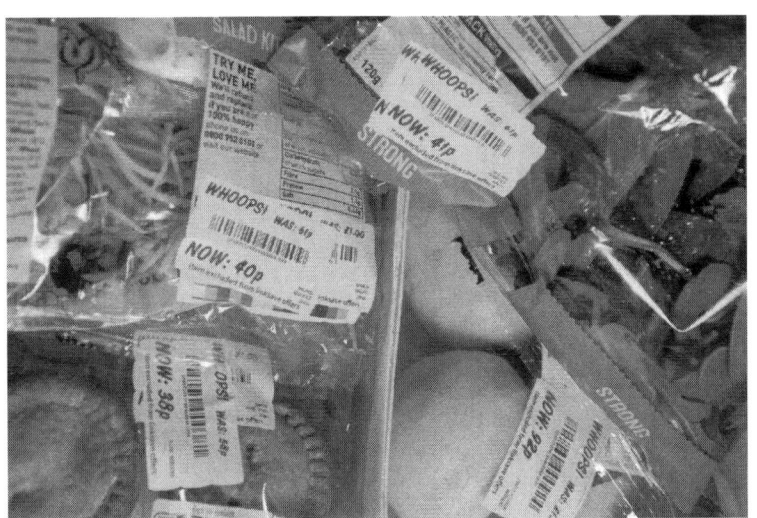

Buying reduced food will help bring down your shopping bill drastically.

Take stock – know what is in your cupboards before you go shopping.

You'll use less cheese when it's grated.

Frozen berries are just as good as fresh, and much cheaper.

If you buy vegetables in bigger packs, keep them in the shed or garage in the cooler months to help them stay fresher for longer.

Buy nuts, fruits and seeds form health food stores in bigger packs – they work out very expensive at the supermarket.

Use that chicken carcass to make stock for soup or gravy.

Vegetable peelings can be used to make vegetable stock.

Serve ice cream in a cone rather than a bowl.

Bulk out meals like cottage pie with grated carrots.

Buy bacon misshapes – they are much better value.

Instead of making porridge with all milk, try half milk and half water.

Don't throw out crystallized honey, as warming it will make it runny again.

Don't buy ready-made spice mixes, once you have built up a good mix of spices in your kitchen you can make anything from taco seasoning to curry powder etc. and so much more.

Don't buy things like sponge mixes or crumble mixes.

Instead of buying pre-sliced ham or meat, buy your own, cook it up and then slice it. You'll get so much more for your money.

Always keep flour, sugar or any dry ingredients in air tight jars. Open bags can attract pests, and if that ends up happening you will be wasting good ingredients.

Save the vinegar from pickling onions to sprinkle over your chips.

Wilting lettuce can be revived by plunging into icy cold water.

Pre-packaged meats are not good value for money.
Cook up a joint and you'll get much more for your
money.

Keeping your baking ingredients in sealed jars will
stop any mites from spoiling them.

Try making home-made ice-cream. It can be made using condensed milk and some cream (you can buy the cream reduced from the supermarket). You can have it plain, with fruit/chocolate chips or whatever else you fancy.

If you need sausage meat, it can be cheaper to buy sausages and remove the meat from the skins.

Stop buying magazines – there are plenty of free publications in supermarkets and shops.

Stop buying fresh flowers, if you love your flowers buy some artificial ones.

Try the pound stores.

Shop around – don't just do all of your shopping in one store.

Get every loyalty card available.

Try couponing – using a coupon when the product is on offer can often mean you end up paying very little.

Use shopping apps. When combined with special offers, these mean you can end up paying very little, sometimes you can even get paid to take the item away.

Shopping apps often give away free products.

If you have a son or daughter at uni or college, get them to come shopping with you. They can get student discount on many things.

Buy everyday items in bulk to save money in the long run.

Stockpile on items you buy regularly when you see a good offer.

If you have any leftover cream, it can be used to make butter. It's worth picking up any reduced cartons in the supermarket to do this too.

If you make butter using cream, keep the buttermilk and use to make scones etc.

Go meat free for a few days a week.

Soups are very cheap to make. Have a few days where you eat soup.

Buy refills of things if you can (e.g. instant coffee refill packs).

Stop being a brand snob – try the supermarket own brands or value ranges.

Meal plan. Plan your meals around the ingredients in your cupboards – this might mean that you don't have to buy anything on some weeks.

Control your portion size. This will be good for your waistline and your purse!

Take your own lunch and drinks to work.

Go foraging, but make sure you do know what is safe to pick and eat.

Make sure you have a good supply of medicines and first aid items. Don't wait until you are ill and then have to pop to the convenience store or garage and end up paying more than you need to.

Try markets for fruit and vegetables. Many traders sell full carrier bags for just a couple of pounds.

If you like a beer, buy a home brew kit. It works out much cheaper.

Stop spending on takeaways. Why not have a themed night once a week at home? For example, you could have a curry night, a pizza night or a Thai night.

Buy baking tray liners. Some can be used up to 1000 times, which saves on parchments and foils.

Buy non-perishable items in bulk.

Before you go shopping, plan your meals around what's in your cupboards.

Reusable baking liners will help you save on baking parchment and foil.

Avoid convenience stores.

Check your cupboards before you go shopping. How many times have you bought something only to come home and find one at the back of the cupboard?

Check the price per grams or unit, as the supermarkets can often trick you into thinking you are getting more for your money, when actually, you are not.

Place a tea towel in the bottom of the vegetable/salad drawers in the fridge. This absorbs moisture and therefore will keep your produce fresher for longer.

Build a pantry of staple ingredients (flours, sugars, stock cubes/powders etc.).

If you have a sweet tooth or buy chocolate and sweets for the children, after Christmas selection boxes can be bought at a reduced price – ideal to stock up.

Buy from online retailers who sell a range of food that has passed or is near its best before date. You can buy in bulk very cheaply.

Get every last bit out of those tubes, bottles and jars.

Invest in some silicone bakeware – no need for greasing or lining then.

Buy the wonky veg from the supermarket.

Cheaper cuts of meat are ideal for slow cooking.

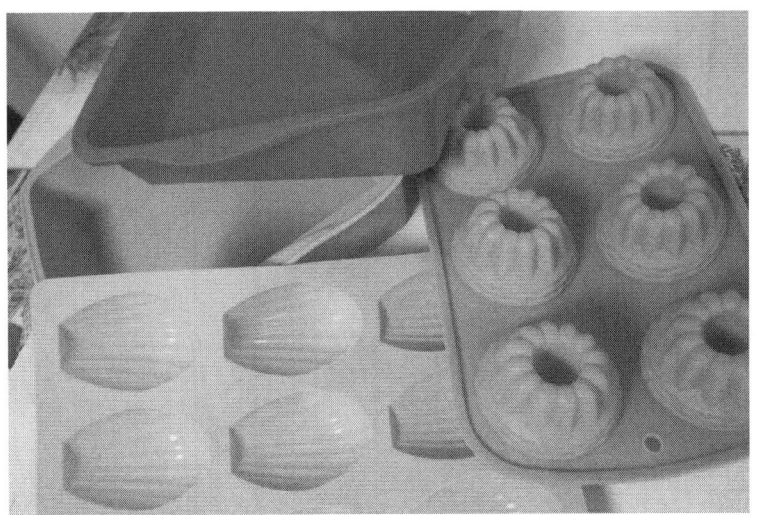
Silicone bakeware saves on buttering dishes and buying baking parchment.

# Health, Beauty and Fashion

Save money on tissues by using toilet roll instead.

Cancel your gym membership.

Use dental floss to get in those hard to reach areas – take good care of your teeth to save on dental bills.

Use a pea-sized amount of toothpaste. It's not about how much toothpaste you use, but about your cleaning technique.

Stop buying shaving foam. A good creamy soap works just as well.

Save all of your old soap slithers to make into a new bar.

When buying cotton wool, opt for pleated – this is usually much cheaper than balls or pads.

Buying cotton wool from the baby section is often better value than buying it from the beauty section.

Cut make up sponges in half.

Buy a solid or crystal deodorant – they might be more expensive to buy but they last a very long time, making it much better value in the long run.

Buy muslin cloths for removing make up, cleansing, toning etc. Just pop them in the washing machine, as it saves on buying wipes and cotton wool.

Applying body lotion immediately after you have dried yourself after getting out of the shower or bath means your skin won't need to absorb so much product.

Use aqueous cream as a moisturiser, it is very good value.

Use the correct amount of product.

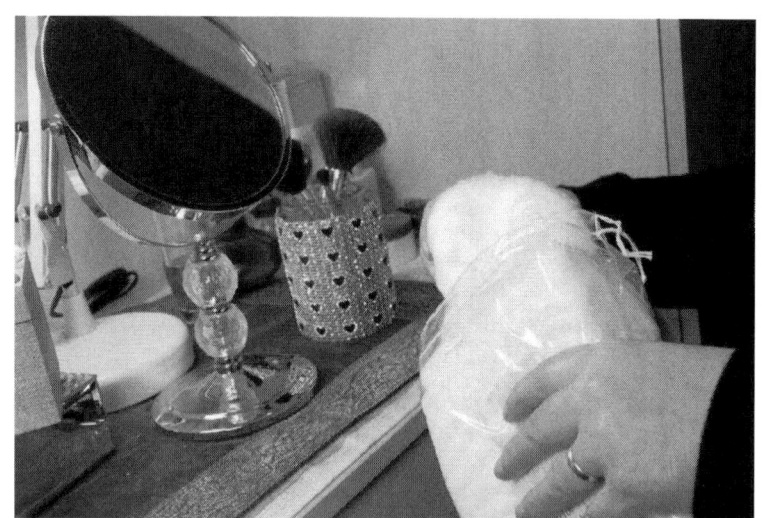

Buying pleated cotton wool is much better value
than buying it in pads or balls.

A pea-sized amount of toothpaste is all you need.

Some well-known beauty brands/companies allow you to return empty containers/pots in exchange for a free product.

Store oil-based cosmetics (such as lipsticks, foundations and liners) in the fridge. That way they will last longer, as fluctuating room temperatures can damage your make up.

Stop having manicures and pedicures – do it yourself!

Many department stores will offer you a free facial.

If you use make up remover wipes, tear them in half.

Ask in the department stores if they have any free samples.

When buying cosmetics, beware of brands – you are often paying for the premium packaging.

Do you really need those high-end skincare products? Using a few simple products combined with a healthy diet and plenty of water can improve your complexion.

Have a go at making your own face and body scrubs – these can be made with just a couple of simple ingredients.

If you have a lipstick and you don't like the colour, don't waste it – layer it up with another colour.

When your jeans or trousers are faded, don't throw them out. Fabric dye can be bought very cheaply, making them look as good as new.

Learn basic sewing skills – what a waste just to throw something out just because it has got a hole in it!

Invest in a pair of hair clippers. They are very easy to use.

Check out the local college, where you can often get discounted haircuts and beauty treatments.

Dye your own hair.

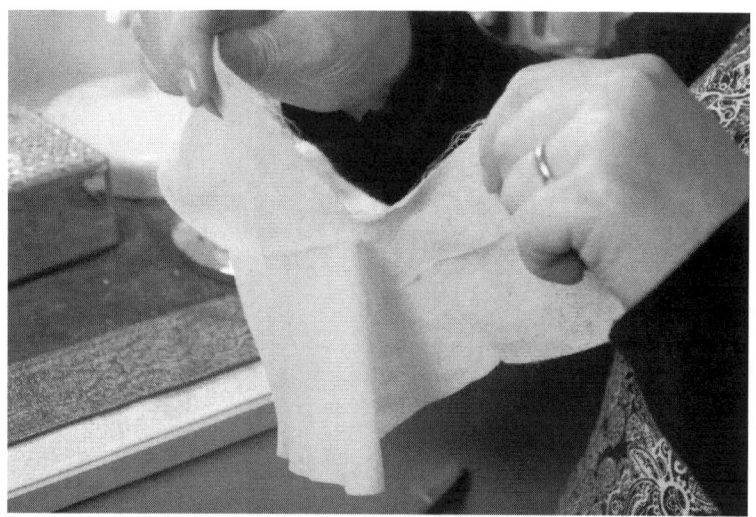

Tear your makeup wipes in half.

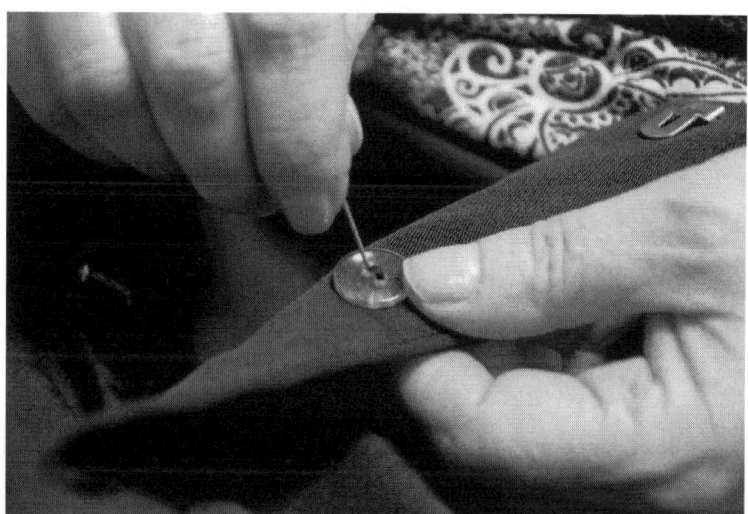

Learn to make do and mend.

Polish your footwear. Not only does it look nice, it will also protect them.

If your need new clothes or shoes, try charity shops, car boots and jumble sales.

Why not have a swishing party?

Wash dark clothes on a cold cycle to preserve the colour in your garments. This also saves money on heating water.

Choose a low maintenance hairstyle.

You don't need to buy brand new school uniforms – many schools have a second hand department.

Instead of buying a new outfit for a special occasion, just jazz an old outfit up with a few accessories.

Don't buy clothes which need dry cleaning.

Stick to a classic wardrobe. Trends are just that – they go out of fashion fast.

Buy clothes out-of-season.

Buy the right size – don't buy clothes hoping one day they will fit.

# Garden

Instead of buying large plant pots for growing crops in, use large builders buckets and drill some holes in them for drainage. They are ideal, as the handles make them easy to carry around.

Get a compost bin.

Collect seeds from your garden or from friends or family, as they you can grow some free plants.

Keep the wire ties which come with toys and gifts, as they are ideal for plant ties.

Invest in a water butt or look for one on a local freebie site. The water saved can be used for the garden, watering houseplants, as well as outside cleaning jobs like washing the patio, windows and paintwork. It's also ideal for washing the car.

When cleaning the fish tank, pour the water over the non-edible plants in the garden.

Try growing your own fruit and veg.

Transform that high maintenance fountain or water feature into a low maintenance feature or a planter.

If you feed the wild birds and like growing sunflowers, there's no need to buy a pack of sunflower seeds. Just use a few from the bird food mix.

Grow your own herbs.

Save all plastic pots and trays from food packaging for growing seedlings.

Lolly sticks make good plant labels.

Plant your own bulbs for indoor displays in the winter months, like hyacinths, narcissi etc. Buying a bag of bulbs and planting your self is so much cheaper than buying those ready to grow planters from the garden centres or supermarkets.

Don't buy garden canes. Go for a walk and try and find some windfall sticks.

Collect free rainwater for all of your outdoor uses.

Fruit punnets and packaging make ideal seed trays.

Save and dry the lavender from the garden and make some lavender sachets for your wardrobe.

Keep toilet roll tubes for growing seedlings.

Harvest your herbs in the summer and dry for use in the winter.

When you are out for a walk, pick some nettles and soak in water for several weeks. This will make a nutrient-rich plant food/fertiliser.

Put crushed egg shells around your veg to deter the slugs and snails.

There is always someone giving away free horse manure – it's great for the garden!

Cover garden furniture when not in use, as exposure to the elements will wear it out more quickly. If you look after it well, it will serve you well.

Grow more perennials – these are plants that live for more than two years. Buying annuals can work out very expensive.

Use the nets from oranges to store your bulbs in. The air can then circulate and stop the bulbs getting mouldy and rotting. Alternatively, just keep the little bags you bought the bulbs in.

Use egg cartons for sowing seeds.

Salad can easily be grown all year round on the windowsill.

Split established plants either for use in your own garden or pot on and give as gifts. You could even sell some at the local car boot sale.

Make mini cloches from plastic bottles.

Grow hardy plants which will not die in the winter.

Visit the sick bay in the garden centre. The plants will be cheaper, they just need a bit of TLC.

Crushed egg shells keep the slugs away.

Freshen up your wardrobe with free lavender from the garden.

53

# Transport

If it's only a short journey, walk instead of taking the car.

Get a smaller car, it's cheaper on tax, insurance and running costs.

Car share.

Rent out your driveway.

Keep an eye out for supermarket fuel offers.

If you are a pensioner, use that bus pass instead of taking your car.

Check your tyres – keeping them properly inflated will help save money.

Combine your trips.

Clean the car air filter. If it is dirty and clogged, cleaning it can improve your cars performance and efficiency.

Drive economically.

Stop using taxis.

When travelling long distance, check to see if the buses or trains work out cheaper.

Turn off your engine when you are stuck in a traffic jam.

Don't fill the petrol tank right up. Fuel creates extra weight, so keep it half full and you will use less fuel.

Use the Park & Ride when driving in large towns. It can save you on fuel and parking charges.

If you fly, try using a budget airline.

When you book a train ticket, see if it works out cheaper to split the journey into sections.

Buy rail and bus tickets in advance to save money.

Get a railcard – you can get up to a third off many routes.

If you commute by train regularly, railcards can come with many benefits.

Keep your bus tickets. They often have vouchers and offers on the back.

Cycle to work – it's free! If you haven't got a bike, look out for one on the local free sites.

# Cleaning and Laundry

Stop buying so many different cleaning products – keep it simple.

Use old newspapers for cleaning windows.

Try making your own cleaning products – it is very easy, you can make them with a few simple things like white vinegar, bicarbonate of soda and lemon juice for example.

Wear an apron to keep your clothes clean.

Buy the large 2 litre bottles of supermarket value bleach and pour into an old 1 litre bottle – you can get two bottles for less than the price of one.

There's no need to buy the expensive mould and mildew sprays for cleaning the bathroom – the thin value bleach is ideal for putting in an old spray bottle.

Don't waste money on bleach to sterilise your dishcloths or sponges – put them in a bowl of water and pop into the microwave and heat until almost boiling, or put them in the dishwasher.

Use old or odd socks as cleaning mitts.

There is no need for air fresheners – just open those windows and let the free fresh air in.

Use less laundry detergent and fabric softeners.

Stop using kitchen roll for wiping spills.

Wear your clothes for longer – if they look and smell clean, you can wear them for a few more days.

Use your towels more than once.

No need for buying extra stain removers – just leave soiled clothes soaking in a bucket of water with your regular laundry detergent overnight.

Wear an apron when cooking/baking to keep your clothes cleaner for longer.

Decanting value bleach - getting two bottles out of it for less than the price of a regular bottle.

Old socks make perfect cleaning mitts.

If you wear smart or good clothes for work, change into your old and casual clothes when you get home. They will last longer and you can avoid getting them dirty from doing jobs around the house.

Use a wipe clean tablecloth.

Keep any old flannels and clothes for using as cleaning rags.

Cut the dishwasher tablets in half.

If you get a hole in one of your rubber gloves, don't just throw them out – keep the good one, then eventually you will be able to make another pair.

If you use wipes for cleaning around the toilet, use value baby wipes instead.

A wipe-clean tablecloth saves washing fabric ones.

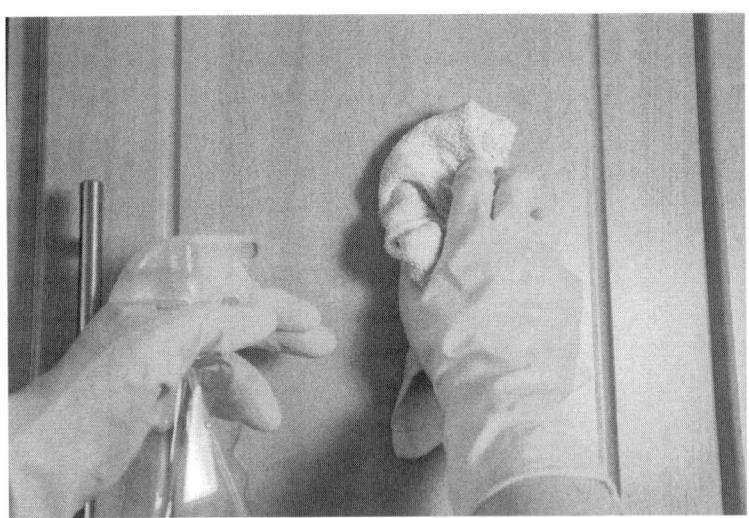

Old flannels or rags are ideal for all of your cleaning jobs.

## Miscellaneous

Make a list of all of your incomings and outgoings.

Set yourself a budget and stick to it.

Reuse gift bags, paper and bows.

Recycle greetings cards – use them to make new cards.

Make gift tags from old cards.

Keep any ribbons for making gift tags. Even the ribbons you find in the shoulders of jumpers and tops can be used.

Take your own popcorn and snacks to the cinema.

Take cuttings from your houseplants and when they grow into a nice plant, they can be used for a gift.

Stop buying freezer labels – just write on freezer bags instead.

Cancel any magazine subscriptions.

You've heard the saying 'see a penny, pick it up' – don't be embarrassed, just do it! It's surprising how much money you can find over the course of the year.

Get as many free samples as you can from freebie sites.

Join the local free sites, it is amazing what you can find.

Stop buying newspapers – you can listen to the news on TV or read online.

If you use public transport, pick up any newspapers and magazines which have been left behind. They will only get thrown out.

No need to waste money on freezer labels – just use a marker pen.

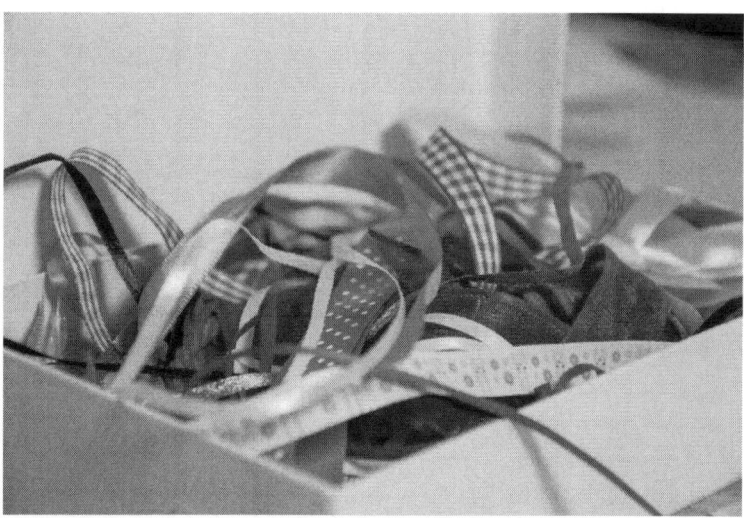

Save ribbons from your craft work and use them for gift tags.

Make sure you don't leave posting cards and gifts until the last minute – post them second class.

Try using couriers for parcels, as they usually work out cheaper than the normal postal services.

Leftover wallpaper is ideal for wrapping gifts.

If you see something which you can make good use of in a skip, don't be shy. Ask if you can have it!

Decant things like shampoo, conditioner and washing up liquid into pump dispensers – this will help you to stop using more than necessary.

Use shower gel or bubble bath in pump soap dispensers, they work just as well as hand wash.

Reuse cereal bags, bread bags etc. – they can be used for freezer bags or sandwich bags.

Try making some homemade gifts.

Shop for gifts all year round, especially in the sales and/or when you see a bargain. Make a gift drawer to keep them in.

Go to a car boot sale.

Use price comparison websites.

If you want a day out, there are plenty of free things you can do; like go to the park, visit the beach, go walking, visit a museum/gallery, attend local events etc.

Check out the local selling pages/groups.

Always keep a carrier bag with you or keep some in the car. All those bag charges soon add up!

Learn to say no.

Wallpaper can make really nice gift wrap.

Pump dispensers ensure you use just the right amount of soap/washing liquid.

Switch bank accounts to take advantage of perks –
many will offer you money to switch.

If you go out for the day, take your own lunch and
drinks.

An obvious one really – spend less money than you
have coming in.

Ditch those credit cards.

Stop smoking. It is just burning money away, as
well as being very bad for your health.

Have a no spend week once in a while.

Know your prices – make a price book.

Invest in some rechargeable batteries.

If you have Skype, use it to save on phone charges.

Reuse scrap paper and envelopes.

Get the whole family on board with the money saving.

Buy out of season – i.e. gifts after Christmas, knitwear and winter coats in the Spring sale etc.

Downsize your home.

Rent out your spare room.

Learn to do some basic DIY instead of paying tradesmen.

Don't be a collector.

Wash and reuse grip seal bags.

Take your own lunch and drinks to work or when you go out for the day.

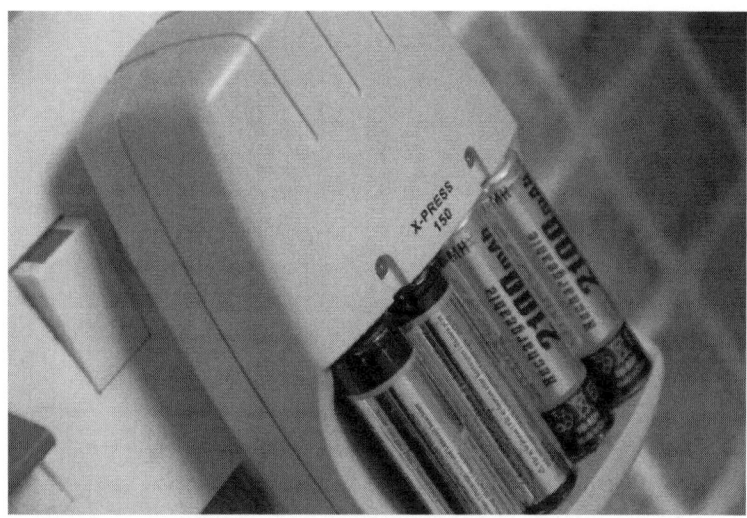

Buying rechargeable batteries saves money on buying single-use ones.

When on holiday, if you have friends or relatives nearby, see if you can stay with them.

If you're on holiday abroad, you usually have to pay to use public toilets, so look out for free entry museums and galleries and use the toilets there.

Fancy a free holiday? How about house sitting?

Stop buying real Christmas trees – artificial ones are just as nice.

Make your own Christmas wreath.

Old comics make great gift wrap.

Don't buy cookbooks – you can find plenty of recipes online.

Use the library.

eBooks are cheaper than hardback or paperback books.

Don't waste a single thing.

Use a soap dish with draining holes to stop your bar of soap going soggy, therefore making it last much longer.

Using a scrunchie or a sponge in the shower rather than a flannel. They lather up much more easily, meaning you will use less soap.

Keep your bars of soap in your clothes drawers – no need to buy scented drawer liners.

Shop with cash only – you can only spend what you have.

When on holiday, if breakfast is included, fill yourself up for the day then you won't have to buy lunch.

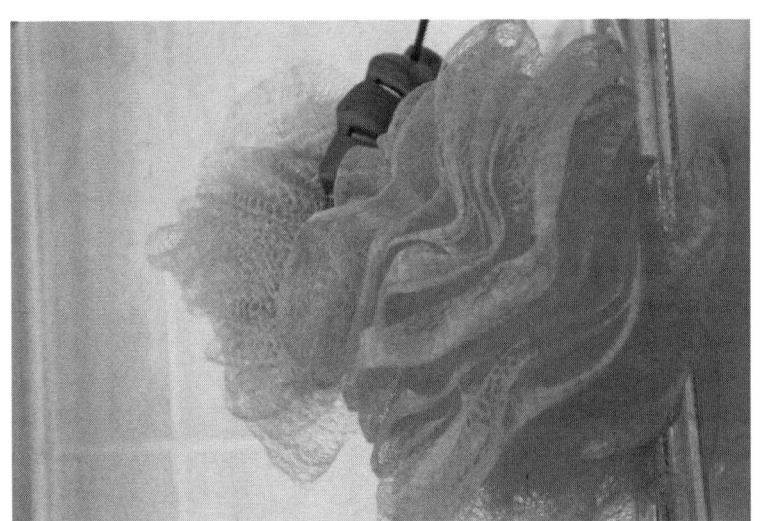

Shower scrunchies lather up very well, so you can
use less soap.

Leave your cards at home and take cash – then you
can only spend what you have.

When going to the seaside, take your own beach mats or chairs. No need to spend money on hiring chairs and loungers.

Staying in a hostel can work out much cheaper than a hotel.

Save up candle wax from the bottom of jars – it soon builds up, and can be melted down to make new candles. Wicks can be brought very cheaply.

If you are retired and have no commitments, it can be cheaper to stay abroad in the Winter months rather than paying huge energy bills.

Use a wind-up torch and radio.

If you have children, accept any hand-me-downs.

Check to see if you are entitled to any benefits.

Don't use a cash point where you are charged a fee.

Don't pay for a babysitter – babysitting can be shared with family and friends.

Cut down on expensive hobbies.

Don't buy plastic food boxes or tubs, keep any empty ice cream tubs etc.

Walk the children to school. Not only is it good exercise, but it is more sociable for you and the children.

If you have a wireless battery-operated computer mouse, turn it off when not in use.

Combining your phone, TV and internet services could give you some good savings.

Stop buying TV guides – you can find them online or on your TV's EPG.

If you burn candles, save leftover wax and make your own candles.

Turn off the computer mouse when not in use to prolong the battery life.

Don't throw away those empty ink cartridges – they can be sold on online auction sites. People will buy them to refill, or some stationary stores will give you money back for your empties.

If you buy wrapping paper, pick a plain roll so you can use it for different occasions (birthdays, Christmas, anniversary etc.)

After you've done some painting, cut down on the amount of brush cleaner you use by wiping as much paint off as you can using an old cloth.

Always print double-sided – then you won't use as much paper.

Run your home like a business – account for every penny.

Don't try and keep up with the Joneses.

Finally...
Be content with what you have.

# Ideas For Making Extra Money

As well as trying to save money, look into ways of bringing more money into the home. Here are a few ideas to generate some extra money:

See if you can get some overtime at work.

Declutter and sell your unwanted items – there are many selling platforms. You can use online auction sites, auction houses, local selling pages or maybe do a car boot sale or hold a garage sale.

There are also several online sites which specialise in buying CDs, DVDs and books. See how much they'll buy them for.

Join some survey sites, as you can earn cash and/or vouchers – the vouchers would be ideal to save up and give for gifts.

Join a product testing site. You will get products to test and keep and also sometimes get rewarded when you complete a follow-up survey.

Become a mystery shopper – you can get cash rewards for completing various tasks in your local area.

Do you have a spare room? If so, you could rent it out or maybe host students.

Rent out your driveway.

Try direct selling.

If you are crafty, can you sell your creations?

What about trying upcycling furniture?

Grow and sell plants and flowers.

Make jams and preserves to sell.

If you are a beautician or hairdresser, get some extra business from family and friends.

Sell unwanted gold.

Do the Free Postcode Lottery.

Could you offer a service? People will happily pay for good reliable services like cleaning, ironing, dog walking, childminding, gardening etc.

# Afterword

By following these tips you can start to live more simply, and appreciate what you have – simple living also makes life less stressful.

Many of these tips will only save you a small amount of money, but over time it can add up to huge savings. Put all the money you save right into the savings pot and watch those pennies turn into pounds.

With hard work and determination you can and will reach your goal.

If you keep the frugal mindset, it will become a way of life.
The rewards are extremely satisfying.

Printed in Great Britain
by Amazon